Get Hired: Give yourself the best chance to get the job!

A simple comprehensive guide for candidates whatever stage of their career.

Karen Macphee

Clink Street

Published by Clink Street Publishing 2020

Copyright © 2021

First edition.

paperback 978-1-913568-53-5
ebook 978-1-913568-54-2

Thank you to my husband Paul for his gentle encouragement.

Contents

Foreword

Over the last 20 years in various aspects of recruitment, I have seen thousands of CVs and screened candidates face to face for their suitability for a particular job or career move.

I am sharing my experience of coaching candidates in interview techniques, career development as well as managing both themselves and other people.

I wanted to write ***Get Hired: Give yourself the best chance to get the job!*** specifically for candidates to give them the best chance in an interview and to give them insight and understanding into what happened when they have not been successful in previous interviews.

You might have chosen ***Get Hired: Give yourself the best chance to get the job!*** because you are taking that first step into the commercial world and want to know the processes of how to put yourself into the job market and be able to market yourself successfully. Gaining an understanding of the interview process from both the candidate's and the employer's viewpoint and understanding the importance of revising before the interview will not be a waste of your time.

I trust this book will provide you the **CANDIDATE** with useful tips and enlighten you. Most of all it will provide you with the belief and confidence that **YOU** can achieve the best chance possible of securing the **JOB** you want.

Good luck!

Karen Macphee
www.kmccoaching.co.uk

Chapter 1
Employers

Why do employers put themselves and their companies through the recruitment process?

There are many reasons for a company wanting to recruit more employees: staff leaving, economic changes, company growth resulting in new positions. Recruitment for any reason is time consuming and costly. Recruitment carries a risk, so the company looks to minimise that risk.

Let's deal with the employee that has left: who is going to fill that role? Will an existing employee have to cover that role as well as their own position? Can two jobs be efficiently worked as one? What has to be put on hold? What effect does that have on the company's productivity or the morale of the department.

Due to company growth that has resulted in creating new positions: will the company be able to fill the roles in-house? If so, that would create a vacancy in another area. Having vacant positions halts growth. All that affects the company's bottom line financially.

Recruitment is not only time consuming but costly: it takes resources to manage the recruitment process as well as time to source the right candidate for that particular job. If there is not a designated HR (Human Resources) department to manage the whole process, the responsibility then falls on to the directors or managers and that has to be managed alongside all their other daily duties. It takes a candidate six months to be fully bedded into the job. Time is money.

Ultimately, the company wants to lower its risk when choosing a candidate. With the best will in the world, and following all the correct selection processes during recruitment, there are no guarantees. So, the employer or company will assess those risks when selecting a candidate, through asking questions to ascertain: Whether the candidate will manage the job? How soon will they see the job/role being managed effectively? When will the candidate begin to add value to the role? Will the candidate meet the company ethos? Will the company's recruitment investment be rewarded?

All these thoughts are in the interviewer's mind when they are interviewing YOU.

Chapter 2
CVs

I know as soon as I see and read a CV why that candidate was not offered the interview.

I will offer you my experience on how to give yourself the best chance to get the job.

Creating a memorable CV

I have seen it all, different fonts, design layout, choice of paper colour. You will need to adapt your CV accordingly depending on the recruitment company used or which job board hosting site you have loaded your CV onto.

Arial font in a reasonable size (suggest 10/12 point), with black type on white paper is the norm. The recipient can always increase the size for ease of reading.

Your CV is your marketing window, you have to blow your own trumpet, as no one else will.

Take your time
A CV is the marketing document for your career, just as a brochure is a marketing document for a product or service.

Companies put careful thought and consideration into each and every word that goes into marketing copy and you should do the same in your CV. Your words need to tell your career story to showcase you in a powerful way, in a perfect world, these things would not matter, but in the reality of the job search market today, they matter a great deal. Be wise – stop and give some thought to the words you choose.

Please don't start by saying, "I am trustworthy and honest" because it is assumed you are – you are not going to say, "I am the world's worst at time keeping."

Remember it is not one size CV fits all. The CV needs to reflect your experience and career skills, especially those skills set out in the job specification.

If you are able to supply a covering letter that can highlight specific areas showing you have the experience set out in the role description. However, with more recruitment conducted through an electronic process that can restrict your CV content, and also reduce your opportunity to add a covering letter.

Ask a person you trust to read your CV. Then ask them the question, "What impression did you get from the CV about my experience?" and "How would you describe my career roles?" That will tell you if your CV actually tells the correct story about your career.

How do I create a memorable CV?
Creating a memorable CV involves time, focus, wording, design and content selection. To achieve a career marketing document that wins interviews, all areas must be spot on and consciously used in the most effective manner. One of

the most common mistakes candidates make when writing their CVs is not paying attention to strategy, word selection, grammar, spelling. For example, if you are applying for an administration role you have to demonstrate you have a good eye with proofreading in all these areas!

Words!!!

There are actually words that can have a detrimental impact on the effectiveness of the CV. The majority of candidates don't consider word choice because they are primarily concerned with getting down the basic information. Wording is critical and using the wrong one can impact your CV.

Read your personal statement out loud, imagine these words used in a TV advert – would it encourage you to buy the product? Ask someone you trust to read your CV and offer you their critique. What does it convey to them? Have you used words that are in the job application?

A recruiter, manager or employer sees hundreds of CVs. CVs begin to look and read the same.

Here are some words and phrases to use sparingly:

- Excellent communication skills
- Strong work ethic
- Personable presenter
- Detail-oriented

Candidates feel they need to communicate their soft skills to the employer because they believe they are the traits that make them unique, but that couldn't be further from the truth. Soft-skills are so common that little attention is paid to them.

Do not overuse tired phrases. After all, no one will write that they take long lunches, is lazy and argues a lot with their peers! It is much more effective to write a description that is action-based and demonstrates these abilities rather than just laying claim to them. For example, rather than just stating you are an 'excellent presenter', you could say "Developed and presented XX presentations to prospective clients resulting in XX new accounts, totalling £XXX in new revenue."

Be mindful that a CV is more than a list of facts, you need to speak about your responsibilities, skills and most importantly achievements. It is crucial to demonstrate how your experience is relevant to the job you are applying for.

Remember to be ready to back up any claims you have made. Can you prove it?

Fail to prepare – prepare to FAIL
Remember what was said in the beginning – lack of company research, or failing to learn a little about the company before the interview, you will be one of the 99.9% that have not been invited for a second interview or offered the job, you will then wish you had prepared more!

Now is the time to reflect, why do you want to work for this company? Just focusing on the remuneration package being offered is never enough.

For example: the working week is usually between 35 and 40 hours. There are eight bank holiday days in England and Wales, nine in Scotland and ten in Northern Ireland. Holiday leave is likely to be four to eight weeks. At the lower boundary you are looking at 42 lots of 35 hours = 1470 hours. At the upper boundary 47 lots of 40 hours = 1880 hours.

Whichever total you look at that it is a massive amount of time that you will be spending working for the company, and that is before adding travelling time if required.

If your daily travelling time is an hour each way = two hours daily or ten hours extra per week. That is an extra day travelling per week. An extra 420 hours annually on top of your working hours.

WOW!! That illustrates why you need to select a company you really want to work for!

Age, health, appearance
With an ageing population, more and more candidates fear age discrimination as retirement looms. They feel they can counter that perceived hurdle by giving a description of their age or health. However, that can be the reason the CV is discarded.

Phrases to avoid:

* Youthful, Mature.
* Athletic, Fit.

Additionally, there is no need to include personal details such as date of birth, marital status or whether you have children.

Passive voice
People who write in the passive voice – come across as just that – passive! A CV needs to have punch and sparkle that communicates an active, assertive candidate.

Illustration of a passive voice:

- Responsible for …
- Duties included …
- Served as …
- Actions encompassed …

Rather than saying, "Responsible for management of three direct reports," change it to "Managed three direct reports." It is a shorter, more direct mode of writing and adds impact to the way the CV reads. On the flipside, whilst action verbs are great, don't overdo it.

These are used commonly in daily conversation:

- "Smashed numbers through the roof."
- "Electrified sales team to produce…"
- "Pushed sales rate by 10 per cent."

I would advise not to use these as standalone statements on your CV, unless you feel they highlight your skills and you can quantify them but use them sparingly!

Chapter 3: Recruiters

What are the recruitment options?

- HR departments
- Head-hunters
- Recruiters
- Speculative recruiters
- Candidate job boards

HR departments

Large corporate companies inevitably have an HR department that manage all recruitment within the company. The manager/director will let the HR department know that they need X. HR will have job role bands that dictate skills, experience and salary. They will place the requirement on either their company website or outsource to a PSL (recruiter on their **P**referred **S**upplier **L**ist). That recruitment company will have compiled candidate lists within the company's criteria. HR will collate all CVs and then provide a selection.

Now the scariest thing can be being told you will need to do a test. Here are a few of the most usual:

- Psychometric test
- Verbal reasoning test
- Numerical test
- Communication test

Don't get into a panic, all these tests can be practised online. There are numerous different types under the same heading however all can be totally different. Ask HR or the recruiter which test they are using. Then, PRACTISE, PRACTISE, PRACTISE and then PRACTISE some more. That will give you confidence and you will also learn lots about yourself. Having greater insight into your personal preferences, values and beliefs will be empowering and can only help you in getting the job.

The selection process through HR can take a couple of routes. A telephone interview or using video conferencing platforms to confirm company compliances. Then they will send CVs to the manager for selection and interview dates and times.

Generally, only for a senior level position will the director take the final stage interview.

Head-hunters

A company or individual that is client led. They usually have a long working relationship with either the company or a particular senior individual within that company. They provide employment **recruiting** services through locating senior qualified candidates that meet specific job requirements. The head-hunter will themselves screen candidates face to face and then provide the client with a shortlist of maximum four candidates. In most cases, a job will not be advertised on the open market if it has been given to a head-hunter to fill.

Recruiters

Recruiters are generally employed by the recruitment company operating on behalf of the client. Typically, they have their own website advertising roles, and they will also search for candidates on open job boards. Once they have compiled a list of CVs, they will send them to either an HR department or the hiring manager/director.

Speculative recruiters

Third-party individuals with no affiliation to the company in question. They are usually individuals or operate in smaller companies. They use generic, open job boards which are candidate driven. Once they have sourced CVs on these job boards, matching the role description, they send them unsolicited to the hiring company.

Candidate job boards

These websites provide candidates with an online platform for hosting their CV. Recruiters or other organisations often pay a membership subscription to these platforms and are able to view, download and (where appropriate) redirect to companies with vacancies.

There are benefits to candidate job boards:

- exposure to companies who do not use any form of outsourced recruitment
- exposure to smaller companies
- candidates who are looking for part-time work
- candidates wishing to work from home
- personal feedback from the market, based on whether contact is made from hiring organisations

One disadvantage to be aware of, it's not impossible for your CV to accidentally land on the desk or in the email box of your current boss. Don't let that happen to you, you want to be in control of where your CV goes.

Each type of recruiter has its pros and cons and not one size fits all. Remember that the same pre-preparation is required in all cases to give YOU the best odds of getting the job!!!

Remember in all areas of recruitment there should be **no cost** to the prospective candidate.

Chapter 4
Preparing yourself
for the interview

Research the company: This does not mean a quick glance at its website. The website is a window to who they are, their ethos, and what they do. Unless the website is regularly updated with news updates etc, it will not tell you the future development of the company. Look further to discover more about the company – use social media (LinkedIn and Glassdoor), e-brochures, podcasts, webinars. There is so much information out there. If you know of people, that currently work or have worked for the company, speak to them. The reason for this research is two-fold – you will be better informed and being better informed will give you confidence. As well as demonstrating in your answers that you have done your homework on the company, it shows interest and professionalism. Would you sit an exam without revision?

Ask yourself the question *Why do I want to work for this company?* – the reward package is not enough. Think about the company culture/ethos, products and services, reputation, career progression, how much they invest in their people, how environmentally or socially conscious they are. Being clear about why you want to work for this company will increase your feelings of excitement for the opportunity. And if that isn't happening you need to ask yourself – is it the right role or company for me? Showing enthusiasm when answering the questions portrays your confidence, and by being confident your voice tonality also changes.

It is assumed that you can do the JOB you have applied for: all employers are thinking *what else* can this candidate bring to the company. Companies are commercial and want to increase their profitability. What makes this candidate stand out from the other candidates? There are always risk factors when employing someone new and the employer is looking to reduce these risks.

You are being selected for and attending interviews but not getting the job – do you wonder why?

If I had a £1 for each time I have asked a candidate who finds themselves in that situation, "What would I have done differently?" and receive the answer "Prepare more!"… Addressing that lack of preparation could be **LIFE CHANGING**. Yes, I know we always say "Better luck next time" but without a change in thinking towards preparing for their interview, the next outcome will be no different.

Well I'm not prepared to let YOU – the candidate – get away with that.

This is where you make **IMPORTANT CHANGES** to make sure that isn't your answer after your next interview.

Think about the job, organisation and your future in the company.

Role play: Ask yourself the question, if you were the employer *Would you employ YOU?* A provocative question! To help put you in the mindset of an employer, try changing places with the interviewer. What questions would you ask the candidate to assess if they are the ideal person for the role if it was your company. What additional skill would you bring to the company? How would you make a difference? That will help you remember all the attributes you have and some that you may have forgotten!

Think about these questions and there are loads more you could add – it will either confirm to you that you want the job or doubts may begin to form – do you want to invest in your future in this company? Either way, a thought-provoking process.

Practise question scenarios: Have three different ways of answering the same question. That will lessen your anxiety and build confidence. If possible, read it aloud, better still have a go at recording yourself. Yes, I know most people dislike the recording of the sound of their own voice but bear with it. That is a good exercise because you will hear the ums, pauses, coughs, stumbling over words and the sequence of phrases. Does the information run fluently? Does it make sense? With silent reading, we will often read what we think we have written. The silent voice in your head sounds different when you say it out loud.

These areas are interlinked to get you really thinking about what your skillset is and your value. Think about the last role that you were in. What was the role when you started and how different was the role when you finished? What had changed? What had you been responsible for implementing? Did you create a process that was more productive, reduced cost, was more time efficient? It can be surprising what you have forgotten and will remind you of the increase in your personal skill development during that time.

Anxious about the questions that could be asked?
Practise question scenarios as that will build your confidence.

Daunted by the questions?
Take one question at a time, write it down in your own language, use STAR – that will help in answering in segments.

The STAR Technique
Using the STAR technique, look through your employment and personal history related to the job. Then craft the answers to fit STAR.

S: Situation	What was the situation?
T: Task	What was the task to fit that situation?
A: Action	What action was needed in that situation?
R: Results	What were the results?
	How did you evaluate the results?

Example

Situation	Give a brief background to what is happening and give the reason why.
	Remember to keep it clear and jargon free.
Task	The work that had to be done/your objective.
Action	Break it into what you actually did.
Results	The outcome, is it measurable?
	How was it measured?
	Where possible quantify this.

Example: When implementing a different programme strategy, the project was completed ahead of schedule.

It has been proven time and time again – fail to prepare, prepare to fail!

Do top athlete's just turn up on the day for their event?

No, they train, train and practise for hours every day of the week.

What do Simona Halep, Venus Williams, Rafael Nadal and Roger Federer have in common? They physically practise to stay at the top.

What do Rory McIlroy, Annika Sörenstam, Laura Davies and Lee Westwood have in common? Exactly the same, they practise to stay at the top.

Practise, practise and more practise as that will build your confidence and that will show not only in your body language but also in the delivery of your answers.

Hearing your voice brings to the fore what is actually being said. Tonality – do you speak quickly/slowly, drag your words, clip your words, is your diction clear? Do you sound confident, enthusiastic? If required these areas can be improved with practise.

KICK "Fail to prepare, prepare to FAIL" into oblivion

Chapter 5
The Interview Process

It is also good to think about the interview process from the client's perspective.

Revisit Chapter 4 about having as much information as possible to assist with balancing the risk scales in your favour.

Fail to prepare – prepare to FAIL
The interview process gives you the chance to meet your potential employer and find out whether you're right for the role and vice versa – but reading between the lines and gauging what the interviewer is really asking isn't always easy.

Now the interview begins.

Your chance to demonstrate your skills and experience.
It is assumed you have the skills.

Please LISTEN to the question being asked and answer it. It might seem obvious, but people filter out words, often because they're nervous, don't understand the question or simply just want to answer it in their own way. Remember this is a conversation between two people, so ask for the question to be repeated if you didn't hear it clearly. If you don't understand the question don't be afraid to ask, a good interviewer will then ask the question in a different way.

> *"Most people do not listen with the intent*
> *to understand; they listen with*
> *the intent to reply."*
> **Steven R Covey**

The six interview questions below could help with understanding their reasoning and what is in their mind.

- Tell me about your career.
- Explain any career gaps.
- Expand on your CV.
- What are your achievements?
- Why have you applied for this job?
- What are your strengths and weaknesses?

What are interviews designed to do? They are designed for one thing: to identify the best possible candidate for the advertised job. And sometimes it may feel that the questions being asked have been designed to deliberately catch you out or make you question whether you are up to the job or not.

But that's not their intention. Some questions aim to establish how well you cope under pressure, others will be designed to reveal your personality or to see what your career aspirations are. Remember if you have done your research and preparation beforehand there is no need for you to draw a blank or clam up.

Remember they want to lower the risk in selecting the right candidate for this particular role.

For students and new graduates

Students and new graduates have to start somewhere if they want to become part of the workforce.

"I haven't got any experience in the commercial world as I have only just finished full-time education." It is appreciated not having the experience of the business world can be daunting, but preparing yourself as much as possible will reduce those nerves,

"I can't give examples in the workplace." It doesn't matter – just take a look at each question and think about situations where you have arranged a party, holiday, out of school clubs, university activities, Student Union etc. You can demonstrate project management, organisational skills, managing deadlines, financial planning, people skills, self-motivation.

You are at an advantage as you have just left an institution where having to submit written projects and experience of exams has been plentiful.

During my time coaching graduates, apart from all the advice included here in *Get Hired: Give yourself the best chance to get the job!* I advise graduates to have a professional IP address. Social media is used more and more by companies to view candidates' social platforms. Remove anything that would portray you in an unfavourable light. A simple business card with name, email and contact number. Even with today's technical communication, business cards are still very useful, easy to give out and easy to keep. When going to a networking event, or a business conference, add the date on a couple of your cards. Likewise, if you are given a business card write the date on it to aid future memory.

Chapter 6
Getting the interview

You have received the call or email inviting you for an interview.

Now make sure you ask these questions – either to your recruiter or, if dealing direct, with HR or the hiring manager.

- What type of interview – telephone, video conferencing platforms, face to face?
- Who is taking the interview and what is their position in the company?
- Is the interview outsourced? Recruitment department?
- What are the interview stages?
- What is the company name, location?
- Is there a detailed job description?
- What qualifications are required?
- What is the lead time to employment?
- What is the salary band?
- Interviews are designed to do just one thing: identify the best possible candidate for the advertised job.

Face to Face interview

As soon as a candidate walks into the room, I notice their behaviour and body language. Five minutes into the interview it is clear why a candidate wasn't invited back for a second interview or offered the job.

Dress code? All clothes should be clean and appropriate for the workplace. Shoes clean. Please, please, leave the chewing gum out of your mouth. Sticking it at the back, or side, of your mouth will not work because when you speak it can still be seen! It is really off putting for the person sitting opposite!

Find out where and how to get to the company. Plan the travel time, train times. Do a test journey at the same time as the planned interview. Also think about travel time in peak hours.

Things to take:

- Copy of your CV.
- Copies of certificates – just in case.
- Copies of documents you have been asked to bring with you.
- Notepad and pen – in case you wish to take notes.
- The list of questions that you want to ask.

All the above can be placed on the desk at the side of you. Most often you will not need them, even your list of questions as you **will** know them by heart. When the interviewer asks, "Do you have any questions?" you can impress them by saying, "Oh yes, I have questions listed, but during the interview you have answered all my questions clearly and satisfactorily, thank you." This indicates you have taken the time to make your preparations.

Please do not arrive any more than ten minutes before the interview time. Why? Knowing that someone has arrived twenty minutes or more early can put the interviewer's time schedule under strain as they also have planned their time. Use the time in the reception area while waiting to take in your surroundings.

You are called in – take three deep breaths, smile, as you walk in hold your hand out ready to shake hands. Now a big HATE: limp, wet or clutching at the fingertip handshakes. The palm should be slightly open, the shake firm (not trying to break or show how strong you are), the hand covering the whole of the palm. All handshakes whatever the gender should be firm.

Sit firmly with both your bottom and back against the back of the seat, feet and knees neatly together. No slouching, twisted body with arm slung across the back of the seat – all bad body language!

Remember your facial expressions. Speaking with a smile. It is surprising how many of us do not smile – possibly due to nervousness.

So, you are the interviewer – the candidate walks into the room, their dress is a bit untidy, handshake weak, they give a mumbled greeting, stand with a drooping posture, sit with a slouch in the chair. What impression are you the interviewer getting in that first 90 second meeting?

Personality
With the best will in the world – not everyone gets on with everyone else. In a face to face interview with the line manager you would be working with, that person will subconsciously be asking themselves, can I work

with this person? Will their temperament fit in with the team?

People buy from people
As soon as you walk into that room, the interviewer will have formed an impression. During the interview they will either confirm that their first impression was right or, during the interview, will have changed their original view through your body language, your approach in answering the questions and your personal demeanour.

What is body language? How your body portrays you to the world.

How you stand: Do you know of someone who you think of as tall, but in fact they are normal height? How often are the people we see on the TV and films shorter than they appear. That could be due to how they dress, confidence within themselves and how they hold themselves. All these behaviours go towards giving an impression of being taller, because people see the personality not the height.

Telephone or Video Conferencing Platform Interview

There is no excuse for not planning for this just as meticulously as if it were a face to face interview. All the rules are the same.

Preparation is key.

You will have had pre-knowledge of the day and time of the call.

Take the call in a place where there will be no interruptions

– if possible, ask a friend to dog sit or have the children. Put the cat out of the room. For video conferencing platforms have the background uncluttered. Have peace and be calm.

Have a space where you can take notes, it is not cheating to have created prompt notes and have them where you can see them.

It is a fact, if **you smile your voice does not sound grumpy** on the contrary a smile can be heard down the line.

Listen, please really listen to the question. Don't be afraid to ask for a question to be repeated. Regional accents can make it tricky to hear clear diction.

Answer the question. If quick enough write the question down, now answer the question asked. So often the question is not answered, the candidate answers what they think the interviewer has asked because, when listening, they are not really listening, but have short-circuited the question.

At the end of the call:

Ask: Will there be a second interview? What is the time schedule for the second interview?

Will there be feedback from this interview– from whom? Time schedule?

Thank them for the opportunity for this telephone or video conferencing platform interview.

Different types of interview

How do competency-based interviews differ from normal interviews?

Normal interviews (also called unstructured interviews): Essentially a conversation where the interviewer asks a few questions that are relevant to what they are looking for but without any specific aim in mind other than getting an overall impression of you as an individual. Questions are fairly random and can sometimes be quite open.

For example, a question such as "What can you offer our company?" is meant to gather general information about you but does not test any specific skill or competency. In an unstructured interview, the candidate is judged on the general impression that they leave; the process is therefore likely to be more subjective.

Competency-based interviews (also called structured or behavioural interviews): Are more systematic, with each question targeting a specific skill or competency.

The word competency can throw you, think instead of your skills, ability, capability.

Problem solving: The role requires problem solving – your ability is that you approach problems by breaking them down systematically and evaluating them objectively so your strength (competency) is critical thinking.

OR

Analytical thinking. This refers to your ability to apply logic to solve problems and to get the job done.

Example: The role is client service based. Your ability is to make pragmatic judgments based on practical thinking and your previous experience so your strength (competency) is common sense as you approach situations.

Example: The role is results focused, your ability is attention to detail in order to produce high quality output, no matter what the pressures, your strength is detail orientation.

OR

You maintain a strong sense of focus on results, driving tasks and projects to completion, your strength is results focused.

Through using specific competency (strengths) questions relating to the role required these competency words will have been used in the job description. With each question carrying a score, and as all candidates selected will be asked the same question that provides the company with a comparison between the scores from each candidate.

Typically, the question starts with "Tell me when…" or "Describe a time…"

The interviewer is wanting to hear an example of a time relating to the question.

Role Play

Usually a second interview.

Being asked to take part in a role play situation either over the phone, video conferencing platforms or face-to-face can for some cause anxiety, possibly even scare the candidate so much that they cancel the interview! To help manage these feelings having an idea of the format for role playing could help with easing these concerns. You will be informed that a role play will be part of the interview process. You will be told the set-up, either over the phone, video conferencing platforms or face-to-face and the approximate length of time for the role play. You will be given information of the subject scenario and the questions relating to the role you are applying for. You will be allowed time to prepare and to make notes. They wish to establish a greater understanding of depth of skills required for the role and how you would handle a situation. For example, part of the role might be customer service and handling incoming customer calls. The scenario might be: you have a customer with a difficult query or complaint, how would you handle that call? The role might be managing a team; the question could be how would you manage a challenging member of that team? Please remember the purpose is to gain more understanding of your experience and skills that would be required for the role you are applying for.

Use today's technology and ask a trusted person to practice with you, videoing your role play. YouTube is another good source to visually see different scenarios. Practise, practise to become as familiar with role play as you would be in attending an interview.

Presentation

Being asked to do a presentation, can be another area that can be daunting causing the same anxieties as mentioned in role play. Remember you will be given a time schedule for preparation, advised the time length of the presentation, instructions on the content, and how the presentation delivery will be given, some options could be PowerPoint, flipchart, handouts.

A suggested rule for a presentation is to divide it into three sections.

First, to overview what you are going to tell the audience. Working on this first section. Break it down into paragraphs/images, data etc.

Second, this is the main part of your presentation. Bring depth of information, knowledge and clarity to the paragraphs you mentioned in the first section.

Final section, you are bringing the presentation to a close, by telling them what has been covered and the conclusion. End by thanking your audience.

Closing the interview

What are your salary expectations?

That is a question I would not expect until the second or third stage interview, so answer it with caution. You should have done some research into the average salary and remuneration that this type of position will pay. I would suggest you try to deflect the question by turning it around and asking the interviewer about the salary on offer.

Typically, they will start with a lower figure than they are prepared to offer because they want to keep their costs down. So, if you are pressed to give a number, it's best to give a range to avoid pricing yourself out of contention.

For example: I'm sure whatever salary you're paying is consistent with the rest of the market average.

However, if the role is for sales, this question could be used to see how comfortable you are in negotiations and closing the deal, so proceed with caution.

The interview is clearly coming to a close, ask about the timeline for when the position is to be filled.

Thank the interviewer and, if you want the role, say so and that you would like to have the opportunity to work for the company.

Hand out – for the handshake.

Over the years I have screened hundreds of candidates face to face for their suitability for a particular job or career move. Whenever I have asked the question of the candidate after an interview "If you were to do that interview again what would you do differently?" – nine times out of ten, the answer is that they would have prepared more.

Why? When a successful interview results in the offer of a job that could change their lives – providing increased financial security, moving home or building an extension, starting a family, more holidays, working nearer to home, providing a better quality of life. The list is endless as to how it could change or improve lives – so why do candidates take only a few moments to take a courtesy look at the company's website and think that is enough?

You only have to watch the TV show *The Apprentice* to see how not to prepare for an interview!

Chapter 7
Interview Questions

If you want to avoid an interview disaster listed below are a selection of the most common of the hundreds of questions used and ones that might cause candidates to flap or become tongue-tied.

- Tell me about yourself.
- What made you choose this career?
- Why do you want to leave your current post?
- What do you know about our organisation?
- What can you bring to this company?
- What are your strengths/weaknesses?
- What do you think our company can bring you?
- How can you help us develop?
- How do you see yourself in five years?
- What are you most/least proud of?
- If you had to start your career all over again, what would you change?
- How would you describe your leadership skills?
- Do you prefer to work on your own or as part of a team?
- Who do you regard as your role model?
- If you had to invite three famous people (alive or dead) for dinner, who would you choose and why?
- What are you most passionate about?

- How would colleagues/friends describe you?
- How can you convince me that I can trust you?
- What skills do you need to develop most?
- What is the biggest mistake that you have made and what did you learn?
- How do you handle stress?
- How do you handle pressure?
- What makes you angry?

One candidate who wanted to make sure they were prepared had three answers to each question they thought they would be asked. They wanted to be able to answer the question within different situations, and that gave them confidence knowing they had prepared. If you were sitting an exam you would revise, wouldn't you? It is exactly the same mindset – preparation. Oh, and yes – they were offered the job.

Read your answers to the questions out loud, it is really interesting to find out all the little words missed – is, it, if, and, etc. When we read silently, we read what we are thinking and not what we have written. Also saying the words out loud highlights all the ums, pauses, etc.

Answers to possible questions

1 Tell me about yourself

Translation: Why should I hire you?
This is not for you to start at preschool, they wish to learn about you, tell them about a relevant situation (don't ramble) that happened during your adult life that is not covered in your CV.

This is normally asked as an opening question. Although

that was covered earlier it is the one question that puts a 'rabbit in the headlights' look on candidate's faces.

It serves a couple of purposes. It is an easy question which allows you to relax into the process and get over any initial nerves. However, it is easy to give a weak answer by being unfocused and waffle. Here they are really saying, "Sell yourself to me. Why should we be interested in you joining our company, what risk do you attract?"

There are many ways of answering that, but a good structure is a strong starting statement followed by a brief career overview. For example, "I'm a senior project manager with over ten years' experience of running large complex projects in the commercial sector." Then how you got there. "I started studying project management as that would expose me to all aspects of people management and provide the people skills needed. I gained experience through working with disciplines on various project sizes from there…" Don't waffle, tell an interesting story about how you progressed, paying special attention to any standout achievements or the rationale for changing roles.

2. Where do you see yourself in five years' time?

Translation: Are you going to stick around for more than twelve months?

This question is set to ascertain what your ambitions are and whether you have a long-term plan to stay and progress within the company. It's obviously difficult to make plans about where you might be in five years, but with a little research, you can tailor your answer.

Find out how the company has grown and developed and, if possible, what their plans are for the future. Work your answer to fit in with the company's plans for growth and expansion. Employers will want to ensure they can meet the longer-term needs of their new recruits too.

3. What do you feel are your weaknesses?

Translation: Convince me you can do the job.

The common perception of this question is that it is designed for you to think of your weakness and turn it into something positive. Thinking about it more practically, however, opt for a genuine weakness.

For example: I used to struggle to plan and prioritise my workload. However, I have taken steps to resolve this and now I have started using a planning tool and diary system on my laptop/PC/mobile.

It may be that your CV is lacking something that is essential to the role, for example people management experience. You need to differentiate between a management title, where that person does not manage people as opposed to a manager who is responsible for people management.

Compare your CV with the job description and look at where the gaps are and how you might be able to address that in your interview. Also, employers generally look for self-awareness in new candidates. To be aware of a development need and to have taken action to address that will be viewed favourably. By the same token, an interviewee who claims to have no weaknesses – really?!

4. What appeals to you about this company/which of our clients interest you most?

Translation: Have you bothered to do your research?
Questions such as this require knowledge about the company. It's easy to find out about companies these days, so there's no excuse for not undertaking proper research. Taking a cursory glance at a company's website, when it's so easy to find out more about what it does and who its clients are, will not go down well with interviewers.

Showing your initiative through comprehensive research can also help you to develop your own questions for the interviewer, which makes you look well prepared and more interested in the company.

5. Give an example of when you solved a problem.

Translation: Can you think for yourself or will I have to hold your hand?
Managers like staff who can think for themselves or offer a solution without coming to their door for help every five minutes. This question is seeking evidence that you are capable and to some degree self-sufficient. They may also want to understand the way you approach problems, whether it is through research, collaboration or other methods.

Pick a decent-sized problem that posed you a challenge and describe your thought process and what you did to resolve it, as well as other people you involved. Some detail is important as it makes it seem more real with numbers and timescales, but don't go into sensitive information or minute detail. Always end with a statement of how successful it was: the conference could go ahead, the customer was happy, the partners managed to hold their meeting. It will stick in the interviewer's head and prevent your answer from dribbling to a halt.

6. What motivates you?

Saying money will give the interviewer the impression that you will be off chasing the ££££ at the first available opportunity. Instead give a constructive answer that will help your interviewer understand what benefit you will bring to their business.

For example: "Completing the project on time and within budget."

7. How would your former colleagues describe you?

or

What would your friends say about you if asked?

Your answer will provide good insight into what you wish they would say. Or would you be stumped to answer?

Just love this question – because if answered coherently it demonstrates that the candidate has a high perception of themselves and how others perceive them. Interesting!!

That is a sure sign that the interviewer likes you and is already thinking about contacting your previous employer for a reference. And this is the time when you realise how important it is to choose your referees carefully. So, answer this question in the way that you would like to think your employer or friends would respond.

For example: "My working relationship with my manager is excellent and both of us have mutual respect for each other.

They consider me to be dedicated, reliable and able to work well using my own initiative."

Or the answer to what would your friends say: "I am fun, people know they can rely on me, I am the one that makes all the arrangements (project management skills, organised)."

8. Why did you leave your last job?

Translation: Are the problems from your last job going to be an issue here?

If you are not in a role currently because of a redundancy, the questions are asking two things: "Were you axed because of a performance issue?" and "Is there any underlying bitterness that is going to be a problem for us?"

The best way is to be brief and factual, Due to the economic situation caused by Covid -19 "The company was restructuring and my role within the company was one of 40 which were made redundant." If they want more detail they'll ask. If you offer lots of justification, it will come across as though you are hiding something. Never get drawn into criticising your previous company or boss, even if the temptation is great.

If you are still with your company the question is more likely to be "Why do you want to leave your current job?" and is basically asking if there are any problems that are going to be an issue in your new company. Never cite any personal differences or bad mouth your present or previous company. A reasonable answer could be "I've had an enjoyable and successful five years at X company but feel that I'd like to change organisations as I am now ready to take on new challenges and gain experience of a different culture/sector."

You may also want to state the reasons why you are attracted to the new company. Career opportunities: "I learned a lot from my previous employer and enjoyed my time there. However, promotional opportunities were few and far between and I am keen to advance my career sooner rather than later."

9. What are your strengths?

When asked that the mind often draws a blank. Most of the time the everyday skills needed to do the role that you are in come to mind. However, there are hidden skills that can be masked. So, to help you identify them, here are a few strengths and how these are used: Do you see yourself in any of these?

Efficiency: Well ordered, methodical approach to tasks to achieve planned outcomes.

Critical Thinking: Approaching problems and arguments by breaking then down systematically then evaluating them objectively.

Creativity: Coming up with new ideas with original solutions to move things forward.

Collaboration: Working cooperatively with others to overcome conflict and build towards a common goal.

Resilience: Dealing effectively with setbacks and enjoying overcoming difficult challenges.

Strategically Minded: Focusing on the future, taking a strategic perspective on issues and challenges.

What strength or strengths would you need for the role you are applying for?

A question rarely asked, what one skill or strength, if developed in an excellent fashion, would have the greatest positive impact on your career?

Biography

Accredited Professional Coach with the Coaching Academy, qualified with distinction as a Professional Personal Performance Coach.

NLP practitioner trained under Dr Richard Bandler and John, Society of Neuro-Linguistic Programming.

Karen Macphee's passion has always been people; she thinks of herself as the bridge enabling others to get where they wish to be.

With four men in the family, all with a passion for cars, it is not surprising she is also a keen follower of the F1 series!

www.kmccoaching.co.uk

Acknowledgements

I have been fortunate in having support in bringing this book to reality:

Carol Elsasser together with her marketing experience also tamed my scatter gun approach of apostrophes and my overuse of grammar.

Kerensa Howset for sharing her invaluable insight into her own recruiting experiences.

Julie Richards for her unfailing encouragement and support.

Nicola Fisher, who shared her experiences through her redundancy challenges.

For all the candidates I have coached for their dedication and commitment and for getting hired for the jobs they wanted.

What people are saying about Get Hired

This book will empower you and fill you with confidence when going for that all-important interview. With her vast experience of recruitment and passion for helping others, Karen has shared her winning formula in an easy to understand format. It is a manual for success!

J. Richards, Senior Manager, Business Owner

From the first time I read this book by Karen, I knew that it would prove a success in helping her clients reach their true potential and achieve their goals whether this would be preparing for their first interview or securing their dream role in their career. Today, as I write this foreword, I know that Karen's extensive experience shared within this book will be an asset to her readers.

N. Fisher, B.A. Senior Partnership Manager,
British Airways

You will get the job with this brilliant book full of expert knowledge to help you get past the nerves and help you feel confident walking into that interview!

K. Howson, Associate Broker

Karen has a wealth of experience in both recruiting and coaching talented people in business. I'm sure her insights and practical tips will give many people a better chance of getting the job of their dreams!

Clare Turner, Marketing Consultant, Lane4

www.ingramcontent.com/pod-product-compliance
Lightning Source LLC
Chambersburg PA
CBHW031615040426
42452CB00006B/537